clear

by Kait Quinn

ISBN: 978-1-7364839-2-3
Imprint: Kait Quinn Publishing

for all those lost to COVID-19
and the loved ones left behind.
for those who have survived.
for those surviving.

CONTENTS

ALL THE LIGHT WE CANNOT SEE
after Anthony Doerr

clouds may grey
and clot the air,
but they'll never swallow the sun.
and closing our eyes doesn't make
the moon glow any less bright.
wet skies won't turn
stars to smoke, and city lights
won't wipe out the cosmos,
only blind us.
even from across town, country, sea,
the bulb on the front porch
calls us home.

EARLY SPRING

Last year, winter dragged her stubborn, snowed feet
straight through white-washed March; toe dipped into June.
Oh, how I yearned for April's dewy wink—
the azalea bush and daffodils, blue

bird trill, honeybee hum, rain shower tune.
But alas, the north was unforgiving;
winter persisted to settle and loom
on the glacial horizon, still clinging

to earth like tongue to ice and bruise to skin.
This year's spring sweeps in on a miracle—
sidewalks thawed clean, sun bright as white hot tin,
rose buds blooming across bared clavicle.

Oh, what promise a year is sure to bring
when earth slow waltzes to an early spring!

BLINDED: A HAIKU

lavender breezes,
mango sunrise, moon in our
eyes—evil unseen

HOPE FLOATS

for awhile, it was smooth sailing.
seas that didn't chop and rock and try
to drown me, choke me on salt.
i was not desert thirsty. i was not
storm cloud heavy. nor cracked soil wanting.
i was sunlight. moonbeam. sprays of lily
of the valley in full spring bloom.
the sound of feathers sweeping stars
into dust. and in one metamorphic moment—
quick as the brewing of a southern storm—smoke blotted
the sky light of my soul. i hit the ground with a thud,
then a crack, blinded by shadow and abyss.
a bird without wings. limp. helpless.

how quickly we fall. how quickly the river runs dry
under the ever-impending, cloud-never-breaking
downpour. how the creek bed swells with thirst
like a parched tongue
all too aware of its own existence.
chest tightens. stomach turns.
arms flail as if they are capable
of taking this body into flight.
i am always on the muscle-tense edge
of the ground giving way beneath me,
hoping that when it does, my back
will have miraculously sprouted something
strong enough to carry me.

and i go on with a desert in my mouth
while the sky bloats and never gives.
i go on rooted to the ground at the shoulder blades
where wings, by now, should have grown.

they say that hope floats.
but all i've known of hope

is longing. the ache of rooting
so deep into the ground, no light in the cosmos
could ever find me. the chaotic search
of something worth holding on to.

MOOD: A HAIKU

go ahead, let rain
pour—i have no use for blushed
blue skies anymore

THINGS FOR A RAINY DAY

banana bread. piles of used books stacked patiently beside the book case. witchy cat puzzles. dusty canvas and drying out acrylic begging for a lick of color, gulp of water, respectively. tiny things, like espresso cups and cross-stitch needles threaded with amber string. and jewelry beads, whipped into patterned submission. ponytails. oversized sweatshirts. cups of ginger, turmeric, and cinnamon sipped in your favorite nook; well-loved YA fiction tugging at your heartstrings, swirling you into a nostalgic firefly-and-moon-beam, summer-night frenzy. piles of blankets. freshly baked cookies. freshly baked anything. lavender vanilla candles. homemade soup. twin peaks, watched for six hours straight. crosswords. poetry. good cries in the shower. dancing without shoes, an umbrella, or a care in the world under the bil-lowed and weeping sky.

MAD

hair storm swept,
skin anxiously crawling, i fall
into isolated madness

IT'S FINE, I'M FINE

i'm fine.
the world's gone to shit,
her children dying
by the masses while the rest of us,
still breathing—thank god, still breathing
—die inside a little
to save even just a single life.
but it's fine. i'm fine.
i'm shaking down to the bone
at some day having to interact
with another human again;
voice shakes on the phone,
skin pools in a sweat,
a year of progress drips down the drain.
but it's fine. i'm fine.
i'm crying in the shower again
over how much i hate my skin;
every pulse, or lack of, beneath it;
how i'm too much or nothing—
all grey, no color
—personality as dull as a blade too rusted
and crusted over to cut skin;
how it could be worse and yet,
these selfish thoughts are all i can think of
—it's fine. i'm fine.
it's harder to love my body.
it's harder to get out of bed.
it's harder to sleep through the night,
sirens flashing red and whirring,
but it's fine. i'm fine.
it could be worse.
i'm fine.

ON DISTANCE

Leaves leaping off a tree. Arm dislocated at the elbow. Discarded petals scattered across the fields. Cobwebs dissolved in the sun. Roots cracking through concrete to find independence from the earth. Splitting of ice. Our shadows lengthening into nothing in the abendrot of sunset. Hello again from a tin can. Unspooling of a playlist, songs plucked like petals from pistil. Lone glove left upright on a shrub branch. Gravity turned repulsion. What once slapped together from across the room now pressed apart like opposing poles of magnets. Spilling an ocean between us with nothing but a tear duct. Leaving behind decayed pieces of my heart. Horizon only ever as close as a mirage.

STAYING INSIDE

staining the walls with juice from the peaches
i cannot stop eating six months out of season.

if July will not come to me bee humming,
telephone wire sizzling, i will swell summer

inside my belly, ooze August like honey
from my pores. all the rooms are sunburned

now. floors sticky with amniotic nectar. sweat
crawling down the windows. from here, swathed

in these balmy innards, the trees, three months skeletal,
melt into ashen rivers—Styx threatening to drown

these ripe shores when Charon comes to collect
his obols off tongues of the dead.

we will survive this. cheeks rouged with wine,
skin plump on pasta, no one would suspect

underneath we are just bone,
grinning and gaunt.

UNBLOOMING

queen flower
peeling disease
in golden leaves.
no rank, no skin
is safe.

IT IS NOT A ROSY FUTURE

sunrise gifts us with hope
like a budding flame
coloring the dark,
and for a window of time,
the air is sun-kissed bright
and breathable, till sunset
sends misery howling up to the ether.
mother moon will save us,
they scream.
she has to!

it is not a rosy future.
it is not always summer-stained marigolds,
soft and tied neat with ribbon.
some days it's a bouquet of stones
slammed against the chest,
losing breath in the gale.

no, it is not a rosy future,
but we are not yet doomed to suffer
in timeless turmoil.
there is flute song still
in my bluebird soul.
there is violet blooming
between blades of grass,
aquamarine spilling through the ash.
and as long as the stars continue to shine,
there is still hope yet.

A FEW NOTES ON HOPE

Drinking in moments:
brief sips of sunshine,
irises gleaming behind rain-speckled windows,
the melodic piano keys suppressing the weight
of this silent storm's dense
and deadly center—
anything but calm;
looking, with hunger and without
discrimination,
for weak or supple lungs to rot.
This is all we can do:
capture light-stained moments like butterflies
landing in our palms.
We, too, will grow wings flamed in orange,
and rise from the grey ash
into our greenest summer yet.

AFTER COVID-19

after, i'll long to
sink my teeth into plums plucked
right off the branch, and i
will, without hesitation.
without question of sanitization,
i will lick the juices dripping off
your stubbled chin and call
it a cleansing. i will sink
so deep into your pores, that distance
will be eradicated from
our vocabulary, and our memory
will have always been
conjoined
at bare, salted skin.

THINGS I MISS

I miss sipping on the overpriced Starbucks coffee,
bar seat by the window, metaphors swimming in
espresso and soy milk across my river tongue,
my favorite mid-sized husky tied to the mailbox
while waiting for its human to emerge
with her $4 cup of cappuccino, dry.

I miss the silence of 4 a.m.—the low light of it,
the moon and stars of it, the feeling of being
a ghost among the crickets. I miss
the sunrise dripping through the windows
like blue ink, like pink lemonade, and eventually
like a thick cascade of golden honey—on occasion,
billowing like smoke.

And speaking of sunrise, I miss the heat of the sun
on my back, bare skin of my thighs. My heart longs
constantly for rising tides, salt thick—though it's been so long
since I've slipped on my scales and bared my gills,
I've forgotten how sea foam feels around the ankles.

I miss knowing what I wanted. I miss when finding
new music was easy. I miss compact discs,
listening to one album on repeat for three months straight.
I miss memorizing lyrics off the sleeves.
I miss the weight of you on me; the sound of my heart
beating out of my chest. I miss the way you plucked
your way between my thighs
like my pelvis was laced with strings.

I don't miss my silence around you, how I was always
making myself small, shadowing to make you shine.
But I miss your lips on mine, your hand clasped
around the back of my neck, my spine
braced and bruising against a concrete wall.

And I miss the way you taste, your skin made up of stars,
the way our hearts were so drawn to one another,
they'd snap together like magnets.
But I don't miss it enough to go back. I just think about it
now and then.

LONELINESS STUDY
after Solmaz Sharif

The panicked quack of a mallard
when his partner has ducked,
unnoticed, beneath an ice cove on the creek
while his back was turned.

When Netflix asks
if you're still watching—the words sprawled
over your fixed, ink-blot reflection.

Pouring a bowl of cereal
only to grasp air
where oat milk had been.

A single glove
lying ominously cupped,
fingers spread like claws
and desperation in the dirt.

LET'S PLAY PRETEND

bring me June daisies and July heatwaves.
let cold water be something for skin
to sizzle under instead of shiver at.
send sun to summer my skin, moon to coat
my throat in howls—guttural, thick,
and hungry for blood.
send fireflies to catch in blue-tinted mason jars
—let's pretend they're stars
scooped from the heavens.
let's pretend this barren soil, this decayed
wasteland is capable of reaping
something ripe and sweet, sticky on the fingers.
let's make a picnic of these canned beans
and jarred peaches. let's make a seaside
of this whimpering creek. let's make use
of this dying sun while we still can.
let's meet, flesh to flesh, ankle to ankle,
honey tongue to strawberry lips.
let's make a timeless August of it.

PIERCE THE SKY

steady my memory,
give me white noise to block out
screams of passersby and wails
of sirens, that sound you make
at the back of your throat
when you fake your own death
and flesh hungry resurrection.

remind me what it is to dream.
to make light burst out of a twist
of wires. to make emeralds of rocks.
to make living of the dead.
because if dreams die, so does the heart,
and i can't spend a lifetime stuck
in my own head
with no pulse to spark me into
the fiery rose i've worked so hard
blooming to become.

take me back
to the moment of ignition.
remind me how imagination—
that magic wand of the brain
—and a stash of vocabulary
can make cathedrals of forests
and persimmon juice of sunlight.
remind me how the sea can be metaphor
for soul and simile for the way
my heart rushes toward you, then recedes,
then rushes back for more.

and when it's dark,
pierce the sky
so the starlight filters through.

SPRING 2020

this spring is the dampest,
the one with the thickest air
and muddiest ground
that we may never scrape off the soles
of our shoes.
every day feels soaked as a downpour,
even when the sun burns like a hot coal
pressed to cold skin.

give in to this weeping season.
grab grief by the rain drops
and bathe your cheeks in salt.
do not let this suffering, this pain,
this gasping for breath
be in vain.
ride this endless ocean. look up
and see, for the first time,
stars glowing over city skies.
it is always when we reach our lowest,
our most broken
that we learn to let in the light.

LOOK UP: A HAIKU

and so we look up,
dew eyed and remembering
the stars we came from

WHAT IS IT LIKE TO BE GOD?

it is a terrible thing.
it is always hearing
the rabbit screaming,
then twisting the knife.
it is blood on your hands.
it is susurrous nights
swollen with wails
of grief and unanswered cries.
it is bittering candied tongues
and anointing venomed mouths
with wine and honey.
it is placing one hand over your heart
and the other behind your back,
two fingers twisted into a knot.
it is a pile of crinkled pages,
rough drafts who bore the axe
before they ever started.
it is promising love and instilling fear.
it is demonic. it is breeding relationships
abusive and toxic.
it is promising grace and doing nothing
when the ewe screams at slaughter.
it is a terrible thing—creating monsters
of men.

HUM

a distant hum
sends the world vibrating.
though it should never take
a sky-to-earth bolt of lightning—
a knee-to-neck shock wave
—to finally notice the storm.

FIRE: A HAIKU

fire for blood. gutting
aisles like clearing throats. chok-
ing on ash to breathe.

THESE POEMS

in the heart of this troublesome decade,
poems, songs, voices   s w e l l.
they are alive.

without a tune, we sing divi-
ded. the poet admits
fragment. asserts these poems
fleeting.

reveal honesty, reach
what art should be.

CAT TAILS

in the blink of an eye,
June had burned to a crisp.
like naan left too long on the stove.
like the thin soles of my feet
against the hot cement.
and the birds still sang,
humidity muffled in their throats.
the bees stopped wriggling head first
into the chestnut tree's late blossoms weeks ago.
the hydrangeas bowed their rain-soaked heads,
having sprouted ivory
instead of sunset blends of violet.
and the cat's tail swayed like a reed
tangled in the wind.

MAYBE WE NEED THIS

when this is all over,
when this strange age of fear has tumbled
to the bottom of the strangest sea,
when the ash has settled
and the tears have run their course,
when the air we breathe
isn't a death sentence
and the sun sends our blood
s u r g i n g
once again,
when our quarantined hearts
are dislodged from their brick
and mortar cages,
and honey seeps thick onto horizon,
i hope we meet
on the plasma-wet cry
of a much needed rebirth.

i hope it hurts.
i hope it heals.
i hope we leave barriers collapsed
in the dust. and i hope
shiny pink scars remain to remind us
we can't go back to how things were before:
to broken binds and starving cries,
to less than and leaving
our neighbors bleeding on the floor.
i hope we find love.
i hope we find giving.
i hope we make the sweetest nectar
out of the rotten lemons we left to sour
and bring our full cups up to the lips
of someone who needs it more.

THIS POEM IS BROKEN
after Nayna Minda

this poem

     is   fract

                ured.

this poem is dis^{lo}cated

at the shoulder.

this poem is splintered.

but if you look close
between the lines, you will b a t h e

in r

  i

    v

  e

   r

    s

of gold.

you will find yourself

Winged and UNROOTED

in a field cresting

with wild blossoms.

35

SUNSET: A HAIKU

sun sets and, for a
moment, strips horizon of
everything but hope

LETTER TO SEPTEMBER

and i know it's a
long shot, but i want to trade
blood for stars, pallid

skin for turquoise waves.
i want milkweed that blooms in
the fall; i want our

collective inhale:
clean, clear, danger passed. no bed,
no monsters. no tubes

and manic beeping.
no plastic sheets between us.
just our lungs, breathing.

LOVE IN THE TIME OF CORONA

let's make love in the moonlight,
gulp a slice of the bright side,
pluck fruit from its dark
and ink rushed branches.
let's savor the taste of these
forgotten feelings—at first bitter,
then mellowing to a nectarine
sweet. flush me rose golden,
make apples of my cheeks.
this year came in like a freight train,
went on like an endless winter.
let's set it on fire, leave it roaring,
ringing copper bright like bells
slicing midnight open. let's ignite
all the souls aching to feel
bright and ageless as starlight.

CAROUSEL
after Vanessa Carlton

there will be no clinking flutes
tonight. no purple roar nor golden crackle
at midnight. no busy balconies swollen with fives,
fours, threes taking shape in our unmasked mouths.
how many streets will meet dawn without
the glisten of shattered glass? how many heads will rise
clear come morning, stomachs settled, pupils
unfogged? how many clicquots uncorked, korbels
unsipped, lips unkissed? but i don't mind this slow dance near
the weathered stockings, embers crackling
on wood, our quickening pace melting
January from the frosted glass. the waning moon has nothing
to be sad about. her life is a carousel and so is ours.
every year ends and revolves into the next. we evolve.
we make the best of these quiet, tender nights.
next year might be different. next year might not come at all.
if we've learned anything, it's this. we might as well squeeze
the sweetest memories we can
from the rotten limes the year burdened us with.

THANK YOU

after Ross Gay

for tugging my toes into the muck
of the creek bed. for my shortest winter
yet. how badly we needed the sun,
and you gave and gave and gave it. how would we
have made it through the smoke and crimson
of summer without that glow that kept us
crawling out of bed and marching on?

thank you
for reminding us that it's ok
to sleep through sunrise every once
in awhile. that there is healing in art.
that when there is time for leaning,
there is time for growth, for honing
our crafts, counting our blessings,
nourishing our broken souls with more sleep,
more reflection, new ways to stretch
our hearts across a distance, and a blaze
of stars beyond the brightest city lights.

and so much of you is laced in death.
so much is battle bruised, fidgeting
with unrest. but no blessing could exist
without war, without sacrifice.
and no matter how much we want to wake
the dead, hide the gun, tongue tie and bind
violence to the stake and set it on fire, we are not gods.
we are only humans doing the best that we can
with the blessings we've been bestowed.
our own humanity should never stop us
from trying. we are trying.

thank you for my body,

my home, my love, a fridge filled with food
and days replete with hours to spend stitching
crumbs into poetry. thank you for reminding me
what a gift it is to wake to sun blinding pupil
and praise the fading stars in quiet hallelujah
that i've lived to see another dawn.

CHEERS TO THE DEAD

jaded smiles quiver.
another year rings in like a siren, and there is
no one to kiss
under the mirror ball's glow. there are no flushed cheeks, pupils
alight, only a clearer view of capricornus in the stars.
raise a glass to survival. drink to the dead for auld lang syne!
yesterday was not our last, but who knows what the new year will bring.

TODAY, RUNNING ALONG THE CREEK

after Jimmy Santiago Baca

Today, running along the creek,
I have a lot to be mad about, a lot to pop
open a bottle about,
but the trees won't have it,
       the sunlight traipsing through
       their steepled ceiling refuses
       to keep me blind to the way ice layers
       along the creek edges like shelves—
       bracket fungi gone alabaster.

I am masked for the winter. I could feel caged. I could feel
suffocated,
       but below thirty-two, air cools the clouds of my breath
       to crystals on my lashes. They catch the starlight
       and moonbeams and I am the fairy face of winter.
       How can I be mad, all silver sparkling like that?

This seventeen-degree wind could whip into
a fury, stir the feeling of skipped autumns and wasted summers.
       Instead, it stirs the dead leaves from their graves
       as if to remind me I, too, am ephemeral.
       So I let go. I let go and cling to the feathers of the mallards
       floating carelessly in the freezing waters, unbothered
       by the cold, my intrusion.

Soon these trails will disappear beneath January's snow.
       My run will slow to a walk, then, and I will notice things—
       the gold-dusted berries, the way dusk bruises
       the snowdrifts blue and purple—that I would have ran
       right past had I not accepted the icy, uneven terrain
       and decided it is better to walk.

Moonlight twinkling on fresh snow,

creek refusing to still its symphony,
tree limbs hands-up to the heavens in their bare
grey glory—

Ah, it is a good walk.

PANDEMIC

these waters—horizon wide
and abyss deep—rock, choke,
brine coat our lungs while stomachs knot
and churn, leave us foaming at the mouth.
but we are no strangers
to uncharted seas.
we, built on a history
of surviving storms like these,
will grow skin between our toes,
trade slivers of our throats
for gills, turn water into blood,
make flesh of ash. we,
built on a tattered history
of evolving to adapt,
will fly full feathered
out the other side
of pandemic.

THE HEART HAS NOT STOPPED (II)

one does not simply
lock one's self in for summer.
not after a winter as long
as the four months of January we've had.
what choice did we have?
what choice did i have
but to curl inward, tune
into every synapse my stirring
brain could fire. to put every thought
onto paper until it spelled out
p   o   e   t   r   y.

it was the canned beans
that sustained me, the jarred
peaches that kept me sweet
when i wanted to sour.
and on the days i couldn't help
but rot, couldn't quite end—hadn't
done enough to call it—i used
all that brine leaking from my eyes
for watercolor portraits of my partner,
the cat, saltwater odes to the only souls
who can see: look! i exist! i shed tears!
i am flesh in bloom!

i came into this bare.
shriveled into it. thought for sure nothing
dying could be revived without fresh
oxygen, sunlight. but o, the songs
one's lungs can carry, churn, expel
on just recycled air! what sunlight
one can spark from banana bread
and cinnamon-sugared pears!
o, what petals a lover can unfurl
when you believe you have nothing

to bloom but decay.

                    what blossoms
one can coax from fields believed barren,
if only one braves the dirt and bones
beneath it, empties at the irises,
brews celestial light still glistening
deep in our marrow. it is blood spilling
work but look: how the geraniums
open and close their scarlet mouths
like beating hearts!

SPRING LIGHT: A HAIKU

spring light gathers gold
—cleanse air, coax flood, sprout summer
from our winter hearts

DISMANTLE

love is a place
where sunrise dismantles the heart.
where sunburns shake translucent
off your shoulders
into wings
carrying you to a sky where the claws
and teeth of earth
can't hurt you.

imagine watercolor sunsets.
imagine cities burning.
imagine lines blurred,
then fading.
imagine nothing between us
but atoms dancing.
imagine unlearning
the constellations.

you don't have to ask me
to love you.
i.   just.   do.
because your blood is my blood.
because your heart is my heart.
because your bones were carved
from the same burst of stars
as mine,
as everyone else's.

imagine flowers on the asphalt.
imagine ripping centuries of violence
out at the roots.
imagine setting them on fire,
starting from scratch.
imagine
dismantling at the heart,

trading the shards,
then piecing ourselves
back together.

CLEAR

one day the sky will turn violet
with shards of magenta pinking the air.
and we will breathe easy knowing
the worst has passed—
our lungs are clear.

NOTES

"All the Light We Cannot See" is after the book of the same title by Anthony Doerr.

"Unblooming" is a blackout poem of the song "Queen" by Perfume Genius.

"Loneliness Study" is after the poem "Vulnerability Study" by Solmaz Sharif.

"These Poems" is an erasure poem of a page from James McGonigal's essay "Edwin Morgan: Three Transitionary Poems," published in the July/August 2020 issue of *Poetry Magazine*.

"Carousel" is after the song of the same title by Vanessa Carlton.

"Thank You" is after the poem of the same title by Ross Gay.

The title "The Heart Has Not Stopped" is a line from the poem "Mystic" by Sylvia Plath.

ACKNOWLEDGMENTS

To *Blood Moon Journal* for first publishing "The Heart Has Not Stopped (II)" in their second issue, [in]bloom.

To Amy Kay, whose early pandemic-related prompts inspired many of these poems. And to all of the other poets on Instagram whose prompts inspired the rest of these pieces. I'm sorry that I cannot name you all, but please know how grateful I am for you!

To my Patreon supporters: Denise Reynoso, Aaron Dragushan, Casey Dean, Paul Idiaghe, and Niels Schoenmaker. Thank you so much for your support! It truly means everything to me.

To Carlos. For offering guidance and answering questions as I formatted this book. For riding the waves of 2020 with me. There's no one else in the world I could stay indoors with for a whole year and then some.

ABOUT THE AUTHOR

Kait Quinn is a legal admin by day and a prolific poet by night. She is the author of the poetry collections *I Saw Myself Alive in a Coffin* (2021) and *A Time for Winter* (2019) and is one of eight poets featured in the anthology *Solace: Poetry of Nature* from A.B.Baird Publishing. Her poetry has also appeared in *Blood Moon Journal*, *Polemical Zine*, *Chestnut Review*, *VERSES*, and *New Literati*. Kait lives in Minneapolis with her partner and their regal cat Spart.

To learn more about Kait and her writing, visit her website at kaitquinn.com and follow her on Instagram at @kaitquinnpoetry.

Manufactured by Amazon.ca
Bolton, ON

35391040R00033